Tumbling Lessons

poems by

Michele Riedel

Finishing Line Press
Georgetown, Kentucky

Tumbler pigeons are varieties of domesticated pigeons descendant from the rock dove that have been selected for their ability to tumble or roll over backwards in flight. This ability is believed to be a survival skill that these birds developed to evade aerial attacks by birds of prey.

Tumbling Lessons

*To Dan whom has been there for me
through thick and thin*

Copyright © 2022 by Michele Riedel
ISBN 978-1-64662-671-7 First Edition
All rights reserved under International and Pan-American Copyright Conventions. No part of this book may be reproduced in any manner whatsoever without written permission from the publisher, except in the case of brief quotations embodied in critical articles and reviews.

ACKNOWLEDGMENTS

These poems or earlier versions of them first appeared in the following publications.

"The Interview": *University Professors Press: Poetry, Healing and Growth Series*
"Concentric": *MCV Literary Messenger*
"Zoom Yoga": *North of Oxford*
"Liquid Bandage": *Streetlight Magazine*
"2pm Bankside": *Lingering in the Margins: A River City Poets Anthology*
"Ascension": *The Sailors Review*

Thank you to Joanna Lee and Dawn Leas whom both did early edits and offered a great deal of guidance, support and inspiration in the writing of this book.

Thank you to River City Poetry group for your supportive group critiques over the years.

Publisher: Leah Huete de Maines
Editor: Christen Kincaid
Cover Art: Michele Riedel
Author Photo: Kenny Jones
Cover Design: Elizabeth Maines McCleavy

Order online: www.finishinglinepress.com
also available on amazon.com

Author inquiries and mail orders:
Finishing Line Press
PO Box 1626
Georgetown, Kentucky 40324
USA

Table of Contents

Descent 1

Easter Glow 3

Finding Shore 4

Revealing My Jiddee 6

Polaroid Instamatic 8

Sister 9

Liquid Bandage 10

How I wish you didn't snore 12

While walking into the kitchen 13

Zoom Yoga 14

Hotel Room 16

5:00 at Sandbridge 18

Still life no more.. 19

Mother's Urn 20

Mom, I saw your face in my selfie 21

The Interview 23

Junk Drawer 24

Va. Clay 25

2 pm Bankside... 27

Hampton Bridge tunnel en route to Sandbridge at 3 pm 28

Seer 30

Restless 32

Concentric 33

Ascension 34

Descent

I'm cruising at 29 thousand
feet in a Delta 5004 airbus.
There is a nun beside me—
rosary suspended
from her waist.
With one hand
she moves a finger over
each bead.

We sink toward earth
on tumbling clouds.
Their shadows play tag
riding side saddle
over fields.

Funnels and air lofts
from tall buildings
causes plane to rumble,
speed-bumping midair.

I glance at my oxygen mask,
think about parochial
school, how I learned to tuck
and roll, wore a white unitard
with cinched belt that ballooned
out awkwardly.

How I focused on the statue of
Virgin Mary—prayed that the elastic
buckle would not slide off,
and that I stood at attention in the
multi-purpose room when being
interrogated by Sister Anita.

All those prayers sent to the
ethers on Fridays in the cool chapel—
fervent wishes, angst, love lost,
journeys never taken.

But here next to the exit door
containing a life raft
I would hold them
all—spiraling down
weightless.

She would drop before me showing
me how, solemnly tucked and falling

her habit undulating as she flutters
freely downward on extended wings.

Easter Glow

Peeking into cellophaned
baskets I see
foil covered chocolates
    that melt too soon
in the almost
    summer sun.
Helicopter leaves,
    pinwheel trees
with blossoms of yellow
paper confetti. Dandelion
nettles floating
    on warm breeze.

On the park bench I sit
with tights
    that never fit
quite right around chubby
thighs
  —legs sticking out like pins
in a cushion with folds

of scratchy yellow lace
    as I sweated
kicking the bare dirt
and hyacinths
    with the tips
of my scuffed
white Buster Browns.

Crescent smile
    yellow purse
suspended,
    eyes squint
jeweled sun-tears roll
as I wait—

photo snaps

Finding shore

I lay the Blue Willow plate
on an old oak table,
blue boats forever frozen
in the crackled glaze scene
heading towards shore.

My fingertips trace the delicate
fractures, silver like Sittee's hair,
its curve like her arm that lay slack
on her tummy while she sits

in that corner chair next to the table.
There she can see everyone,
wooden cane propped, ready to steer.

I find a gouge from sudden drops,
and the crack of Aunt Janice's cackle,
tracing its chipped edges — the shove
and jar of 6 cousins.

Before they arrive,
I hear her
calling *Misheah*!
—shows me how to soften
hard pita on old brick,
her steady fingers narrowly
misses flames.
Cooling the steamy bread
with butter, places it on *my* plate,
this perfectly formed moonshell.

She let me wash dishes.
Bowls bounce off metal sink,
chipping off shards as scent
of Joy lemon-fresh permeates.

But, I proudly hold the
rinsed stoneware as its warmth
travels up my arm.
Suds like sea foam lingers
in dishrack dripping
on crisp apron,
bubbles iridescent,
like speckled cockled shells.

Revealing my Jidee

Through back door,
I see tall mint stacks
and tomato vine shake.
A trouser covered leg jiggles,
sends bees swirling.

Jidee rambles up steps,
announces arrival with clang of cane,
his stiff leg upon storm door.
Oyster shell hands grip a smooth red pearl.
He says, *no one can grow them better than that!*

Smell of mint, earth and white undershirt,
sweat coats nubby whiskers.
His brown boyish eyes marooned
on an island of wrinkles
and permanent woe.

No pause, shuffling past,
he rolls the bounty onto newspaper
covered table,
an offering to God.
Derby hat perched,
pipe falls, tobacco spills.

*Slice it-sit and eat
Inshallah!*
He sat beside the pickled
turnip jars
—smoke clouding head.

Knife flashes in narrowed light,
juices and seeds streams down,
pools on paper.
Room smelled of sugar, fresh earth.

Biting into flesh as it dribbled,
breathing in summer,
my skin becomes its skin,
tingling and sated.

I see his face enshrouded by smoke swirls,
moted dustlight—hardened frame softening.
He shifts in his seat—exhales *Saeida*,
breath hums to the coffee percolating,
steam settling.

Polaroid Instamatic
    Easter Sunday/April 1962

Bridge in Bryan Park
overlooking azaleas
in full bloom. Pinafores and crinolines,
matching white purses and straw hats.
our Buster Browns matching, mine curled in.

We pose at the edge of a shadowy stream,
Dad looking at his young hands, gripping
the rail, sister looking out towards the water,
and I looking at her for direction.

None of us looking at mom
with the camera.

        Dad, in your black suit with
        angled shoulders protecting us,
        matching the dark pine saplings
        that framed our background,

        your smile limp like the overgrown grass,
        in the shadow of mom's parade.
        Did you sense our melancholy,
        our fake smiles tired of posing,
        differences surfacing?

Sister

She gave me a tweed hat
too small for her.
I really wanted it to fit—
its angled slant promising
smart, savvy conversation.
—now lost on closet
shelf, collecting cobwebs.

She gave me a pearl
necklace once worn
on her summer skin,
it fell sweetly
in my hand, each pearl
perfectly placed.
Washed aqua, sequined
blues—like bubbly

laughter from prosecco
as we jumped puddles
under shared umbrella.

But our differences
surfaced. My scattered
drops—she precise,
pinpoint.

Each knot a
sharp-tongued word,
snarled
—the pain that we moved
through.

Fibers flexed, found space
carry weight,
each moment intertwined
yet separate.

She gave me hydrangeas
to plant. Together we bundled
stiff branches, buried them deep—
our hands converged,
drew back
sifted through hard clay,
found soft earth.

Reach toward connection
where the clasp joined—
her hand wrapped
my tiny fingers.

Liquid bandage

Brush a thin film over the slit on your papered skin—
    feel the throbbing start to numb.

Shields against   daily verbal scrapes
                                        blisters and callouses
                                        prickles
                                        exposed nerves

I scan directions for
protection from   splintered remarks

lodged so deep
they remain hidden
until the skin regenerates   pushing the sharpness slowly
                                        toward the surface.

Search for   toxic comments from others
                                      places not yet recovered

                                      pummeled layers from sharp
tongues
that have turned red to purple to blue to yellow from deep tissue that
ooze their spew.

Scars that never faded,
alleyways from the past.
My palms sweat as I touch the thick callouses

breathe deeply, revisit. Let go

knowing how proud flesh bridges a cut
and gaps fill in with patience.

While walking into the kitchen

I saw the white hydrangeas
there on the countertop
glorious and bountiful,
unexpected.
In the too small blue carnival glass
vase, meant to take the place
of the ones that never bloomed
over the past 3 summers.
You saw me looking
with sweat dripping
at the glossy green leaves
that bore no fruit.

I cradled the blossoms
to my nose, taking in
their heady scent.
Coiled petals like ladies' petticoats,
each bloom a bouquet gathered
by a slender stem of green
—how I imagined them,
stately borders on long lush lawns.
Had you thought of these things,
of me in that moment's inspiration?
How I would clutch each blossom
with its delicious delivery,
my summer complete.

Zoom yoga

You are eating chips in your
undershorts.
I lie that they can see.
You belch, knees and ankle popping
as you land on your mat;
phone blinking like emergency flashers.

A moan as your shoulder bends
stiffly in cobra pose.
You finally ignore message alerts
as we move into bridge pose
while Abbycat brushes our legs extra
slowly with her whiskers.

The instructor reminds us to breathe deeply.
I razzle my exhale
trying to sound like Lauren Bacall.

We windmill into three-legged dog.
only legs and feet viewable—
look lost in each home video box.

I marvel how she manages, re-images
moves us from space to connection.

Put your head on straight!
I adjust my neck.
She says it again and I laugh—
you tell me to be quiet

Soon, our minds are lost somewhere
between couch and ottoman.
Two minutes into deep relaxation
you're snoring.

Sunlight falls through skylight
softening shadows, muting your edges
In this moment, you are *illumine*,
an angel.

How I wish you didn't snore

I tug the fitted sheet
around corners,
flatten the night's
wrinkles away,

Restless angst

melts beneath the warmth
of my hand—
missing the touch
of your straw hair

I snap the top sheet once
watch it settle
like angel
wings beating,

spilling out time,
curls and cobwebs cling
uneven corners
askew.

Floorboards
dusted, swept
by its movement
our voices, a familiar touch

You a wall
away.

We dream
alone.

Hotel room

The gulf water laps
aqua.
An egret slowly pecks,
its outline obscured
by water as it burrows
deep.

Behind me the towered condos
wear their golden spotlights like
bracelets.
People with their cell phones
walk, faces lit up.

You are in the hotel
room sleeping off dinner.
in the air conditioner's cushion
and lax blue light of tv.

You say *That's stupid,*
why go out alone
to the beach at night?
I looked for you
at the pool!

I said *the breeze is*
a feathered breath and there
is a lone bird shadowed by water
that moves out to infinity.

I walk back as the gibbous
moon thickens the milky
sky,

Back into a maze
of lotion lathered legs
and steel pan drums,
sip tequila
at the bar, till spotlights
lights mesmerize,
sedate.

I take the sidewalk
toward you.

5:00 at Sandbridge

With the long draw of saffron yellow
on our backs,
we see our crisp shadows
as we walk toward the surf.

Knees knobbier, walking
the same distance
as each year passes.
The wind wraps around us
pushing waves softly
slack and loose.

We trudge on,
nudged to balance
sand and surface.
You and I
walk toward another sunset.
Bent forward
you disappear
into foamy wave
and submerge
rocking up and down
with the magnetic dance
of earth and moon
and I follow.

Still Life No More

Teacup, metal strainer and philodendron,
moms painting framed.

Piano keys travel through wide oak floorboard.
Chalky paper background becomes translucent—
her quick veined hands hold the lipstick edged cup.

She sips and peers out her back deck
while birds tumbled around feeder,
and steamy vapors
shadowed the walls.

She slides the plant toward the cup
breathing the aroma of tea leaves
ponders how the three were complete,
ignores the popping sound of toast—its enticing smell
dwindles.

Paint brushes, oils in a row, rips paper from notebook,
she mixes the champagne yellow—hunter green,
—moonlight sonata vibrating through knots in the dark wood.

Tea kettle whistles as she moves about,
blends the colors to a muted morning light
till nails become tinged in emerald green and background
mauve.

Eyeing her work, feeling the warmth of ambient light fill her kitchen,
content as sun pours through thick windowed door.

Mother's Urn

The pear-shaped clay vessel
became a tomb the day I brought it home.
Its porous surface like black coal
wrought from fire holds her ashes
lowered down into this dark space,
The weight of a small stone.

Precious bones ground into
calcium, phosphate, sulfate.

It fit into the fold of my hands
no vespers whispered
dropped into this cloistered cell.

A tabernacle—
there on my dresser.

This deep chamber
has become a crypt of memory.
The inner lining matches the blue
of her eyes that look out
its smoothness a still river.

Mom, I Found Your Face in My Selfie

The exact same
draw of lips
framed by set
jawline—
a gesture of
half questioning.

Tried filtering in silvertone
soft greys, bright drama
of cinema and edgy noir,
but there you were.

Your eyes
pressed into
my life pages
words become
voice.

You say joie de vie
remember joy—dance
sing out loud
to ease that worry line
between my brows.

PJ's and cowboy coffee,
how we painted together
till the sun filtered
through window
in yellow ochre—

while toast popped up slightly
burned and that banana you kept
fishing out of fridge for cereal.

Chopin drifted
settled in corners as dust danced
while morning washed
the eaves.
Through me you look
at my life, so much left to do,
so little time.

The Interview

Shoes, belt coiled, shirts
and ties laid smooth like runways
semester's over—he's home.

Finding old polish
he rubbed into the pores
of scuffed shoes and skin
until fingers ache
into a hard shine.

Borrowed folder
leather pockets hold dust
seeping into tightly gripped edges
of rehearsed answers
and sweaty replies.

Next to overloaded laundry basket,
he stands
mirror shined shoes
jacketed with runway tie
ready.

He spins quarters in his pockets
with a smile like 1000
rhododendrons outside.
Toe tips out
he rocks back on his heels
—Johnny Jump ups
springing toward the May sky.

I watch him leave
like that first day driving
alone.
Puddled in the window,
while hangers punctuate chairs
over an array of jackets.

Junk Drawer

Allen wrenches, keys,
50 packs of soy sauce,
batteries and old Trident gum—
never opened. The chatter
of rubber bands
stuck together through 2 years.
This drawer sticks. I'm caught
in the hair of things I can't replace.

No more shuffling past the scotch
tape, bills I forgot to pay, plastic
baggies, paper clips hung on
to pencils. I'm full of litter
glue bottles and old whiteout
cannot erase or mend.

My son's old cell phones—
conversations sealed in their crypts—
how we want to hold onto
his slender arms, hugs
right before he leaves again.

I empty the drawer,
check for wedged calling cards,
wash clean the debris,
sweep away weighted dust,
as the sun warms the white paint.

I study its angles,
intersections—how wood
holds memory
and within space lies strength.

Virginia Clay

I love the pinch
between fingers and how
it hardens against my skin, flakes
off rivulets of red into puddles
where I stand watering.

My hostas and I are ladies in spa clothes
who gather in Turkish baths,
thirstily swim in rich minerals.
Together we feel its seeping—my
tired lines smooth
while eddies carry bugs sideways
around my feet.

Picking up my tools and gloves
I thrum the earth,
become terracotta cast,
digging deep, releasing slabs
of memory.

An old mini soccer ball, mildewed,
deflated. My mother's gardening marker,
old bottle caps, my cat's mice toys,
my son's stone handprint
when he was 8,

my hand over his impression
feels its years.
I breathe in the clay,
work through the hardness,
mix in moist rich soil,
fold my frail roots into its
sponge.
The clay holds my sins and secrets,
decides what will surface,
what will remain,

while the cicadas waver
weary from the early morning
heat of July.

2 pm Bankside

Quick to his haunches he crouches low—rear up
jerks to and fro anxiously panting
ready to dive in.
The sun beats down reflecting
back in sharp shards
from the deep dark muddy river.

Tracing bank edge with his nose
he backrolls into the crusty mud
sloughing off his city coat.
Splashing in, with only the tip of tail and nose
breaking surface, his head is low
in the murky underworld.
Above the gentle James unfolds its veil
as patterns of current
sweep the geese downriver
to some other heaven.

Suddenly he springs back to the bank
shaking loose soaked fur,
baptizing me with a tail thumping
hymnal and a howlsong.

Hampton Bridge tunnel en route to Sandbridge at 3 pm

The emptiness of what I leave behind unfolds
to the beat of car on pavement.
Concrete walls and exhaust
press into my lungs.
I blend into its paleness.

The sparkle of sun
pinholes the edge,
then rush of blinding light
as I shoot out from dingy fluorescents,
breathe salt-encrusted air.

Passing car shadows dapple,
my eyes lift toward seagulls.
Arm waving from window,
fingertips flit in bay breeze.
Wind siphons like soft static.

Framed by bridge guard rails,
sea becomes bay,
waves rock catamarans,
and in distance, large barges
are permanent fixtures.

Fussy green exit signs
channel cars
as traffic turns into town
bordered by
fields of waving sea oats

where September light
filters gold,
sweeps her skirts
as the day wanes—
full.

Seer

He rakes the sand
paper jacketed.
"Hola" echoes
from under
shadowed hat
as tourists pass.

Moving with precise
sweeps,
his hollowed
body bent over
in a slow crawl.

Hours dribble
heavy drops
of sweat
into his eyes
as he carves,
sifts out debris.
moving steadily
toward the horizon.

Spiraling,
he sculpts a mandala
with measured step
placing driftwood
centrally,
offers it
to the drum
of ocean.

His body circling—
enshrining,
as heat waves
distort
his figure,

his jacket
becoming robe,
billowing.
He dissolves
into its cool
folds.

Restless

Coastal breezes breathe in one window
and out the other, thwack wood blinds
against sill, carry me along
as mattress becomes sea.

Window shades unfurl waves, lap upon lap,
undertow pulls, my feet slide.
Current slams against my chest, as the waters
slowly drain out, slick creatures surface.
Their eyes roll, my arms flail.

Tossed, tired and drowning,
I drift in a dance of seaweed and brackish shore,
A spin of hair, imbalanced—
face bleached to white coquina.

Salt air fills my room with opaque orange,
then piercing light.
Swallows chirp in tangled branches,
pluck strands of twigs and twine.

Ear muffled by pillow—distant laughter
of a party carried on odd breezes. Twisted,
sunken into memory foam, I toss blankets

overboard, peel away lengthy sheets,
sweat, feel the ache
of shoulder on hard pillow.

Doors close as others rise,
sand-grit steps slide down hall.
Seagull squawk fades into beat of ceiling fan,
flickered light, chilled room air.

concentric

she lives inside a shell
cut off, dried up and left
shriveled
in darkness
dead ended backed up
and bumping
right back into her
reflection

spiraling in toward inner chambers
sliding along pale walls
down a hallway
of winding thoughts
she finds an open
window

slipping toward the light
reaching out
one hand on a chair
breathing in
as colors change
and life begins again
roots itself—
hope returns
she starts over

Ascension

Pray for me he uttered, knelt hovered
over pew, held forehead,
breathed in the incense trancelike,
eyes tightly closed—
held snakes at bay.

With the dark coolness of the pews
against my skin,
I felt your power as you uttered

Our Father who art in heaven...

You held prayer badges against
your forehead like earned stripes,
this battle you waged—
to ease your burden,
the never measuring up.

Forgive us our trespasses...

Shielded with the sacred heart medal,
kept me at arms length,
not wanting me to mirror you.

But I found strength in the divine faces
in sunlit windows,
held your rosary fragments,
connected all the pieces,

*...and those that trespass
against us.*

I placed my hand on yours knowing
this was all we would be—left guilt,
the never being enough,

Ascended away.

Notes

Jidee and Sittee means Grandfather and Grandmother in Lebanese
Misheah: Michele with Lebanese accent

*Saeida /I'm happy
*Inshallah/God wills it

Michele is a poet from Richmond Va. who has been published in a number of online and print journals including *Streetlight Magazine, North of Oxford, Third Wednesday, MCV Literary Messenger, University Professors Plus* and *River City Poets Anthology.*

She obtained an Environmental Health degree from Old Dominion University and endorsements from University of Richmond in Education and ESL and then taught Reading in elementary schools for 15 years. She ventured into jewelry design and photography, taking classes and entering her pieces at juried shows.

Michele began journaling at 10 and continued on an off for years and then as is now draws inspiration from her family, nature and life experiences. She enjoys attending critiques, workshops and open mike nights both online and in the rich poetry community of Richmond. She has found that writing, more so than other mediums, has empowered her to find her voice, and reading it instills energy and movement into her words.

She loves traveling, biking hiking, gardening and going to her beach house in Sandbridge, VA. The happiest constant in her life has been playing tennis and teaching or doing yoga when she isn't writing.

Through networking she has found online sharing groups from Ohio to Zimbabwe that have helped inspire and support her writing during the pandemic. She has a blog at wordpalettes.wordpress.com

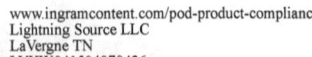
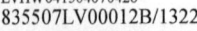